HEM
OF OUR
Hope

Exploring Our Fragile
Faith in a Steadfast God

WILLIAM STACY

WESTBOW
PRESS®
A DIVISION OF THOMAS NELSON
& ZONDERVAN

WestBow Press books may be ordered through booksellers or by contacting:

WestBow Press
A Division of Thomas Nelson & Zondervan
1663 Liberty Drive
Bloomington, IN 47403
www.westbowpress.com
1 (866) 928-1240

ISBN: 978-1-9736-9549-3 (sc)
ISBN: 978-1-9736-9555-4 (hc)
ISBN: 978-1-9736-9548-6 (e)

Library of Congress Control Number: 2020912036

Print information available on the last page.

WestBow Press rev. date: 07/17/2020

DEDICATION

To my grandma Lessie, who despite being born with a handicap that left her unable to learn how to read, has shown a dedication to her faith and to her family throughout her life. It is in her honor her that I write in her surname. - WS

CONTENTS

PREFACE

The Bible gives us a vital but often overlooked command, to meditate on the scriptures. This volume is an outgrowth of my attempts at Bible meditation over the years. The reader will notice a variety of themes, emotions and tones throughout the book, indicative of the Lord giving me the degrees of grace and different truths I have needed at varying times throughout my life.

I hope the contents serve a similar purpose for the reader and inspires you to continue meditating on the scriptures to unlock all the wondrous things God has for you there. - WS

ACKNOWLEDGEMENT

No man ignites himself. We all have sources of inspiration to draw from, and while there was no thought in my head of writing scripture poetry at the time, when I read this poem by George Gordon Byron as a boy, I was completely enthralled by it. What could be more potent than a combination of the Word of God being magnified with the words of a master poet? The Destruction of Sennacherib was the first poem I committed to memory, and it remains a favorite of mine to this day. Doubtless, it has had an influence on my own desire to write scripture poetry. I hope you will enjoy it as much as I have.

THE DESTRUCTION OF SENNACHERIB

George Gordon Byron
"And it came to pass that night, that the angel of
the LORD went out, and smote in the camp of the

Assyrians an hundred fourscore and five thousand:
and when they arose early in the morning, behold,
they were all dead corpses" – II Kings 19:35

THE Assyrian came down like the wolf on the fold,
And his cohorts were gleaming in purple and gold;
And the sheen of their spears
was like stars on the sea,
When the blue wave rolls nightly on deep Galilee.

Like the leaves of the forest when Summer is green,
That host with their banners at sunset were seen:
Like the leaves of the forest when
Autumn hath blown,
That host on the morrow lay withered and strown.

For the Angel of Death spread his wings on the blast,
And breathed in the face of the foe as he passed;
And the eyes of the sleepers waxed deadly and chill,
And their hearts but once heaved,
and forever grew still!

And there lay the steed with his nostril all wide,
But through it there rolled not
the breath of his pride;
And the foam of his gasping lay white on the turf,
And cold as the spray of the rock-beating surf.

And there lay the rider distorted and pale,
With the dew on his brow, and the rust on his mail:
And the tents were all silent, the banners alone,
The lances unlifted, the trumpet unblown.

And the widows of Ashur are loud in their wail,
And the idols are broke in the temple of Baal;
And the might of the Gentile,
unsmote by the sword,
Hath melted like snow in the glance of the Lord!

HEM OF OUR HOPE

"When she had heard of Jesus, came in the press behind, and touched his garment. For she said, If I may but touch his clothes, I shall be whole." - Mark 5:27, 28

The hem of her hope, the end of her rope,
An ultimatum for her life.
A brittle hand grabbed the robe by a thread;
This was it—be healed or die.

She fought the press for a spiritual guess--
The faith that a touch could heal.
And discovered when her blood was staunched,
The power of God, not cloth, revealed.

Likewise, do we have faith, oft weak,
Existing by a thread,
Need also to grope, to reach, and invoke,
A hope that is nearly dead.

To follow a path we know not where,
To step and not see it land.
Try to obey when we don't believe,
Taking that hem into our hand.

We're skeptical souls, but even so,
We bow the knee and pray;
Finding strength to carry on,
From those around us, doing the same.

We all need some light in the maelstrom,
A catalyst to seek the Lord—
A hem of our hope, some way to invoke,
Our faith in God and his Word.

BLOOD
TOUCHETH
BLOOD

"There is no truth, nor mercy, nor knowledge of God in the land.
By swearing, and lying, and killing, and stealing, and committing
*adultery, they break out, and **blood toucheth blood**."*
- Hosea 4:1-2

Blood toucheth blood since Abel's runned,
Through the hands of Adam's other son.
Ascending from the ground to come,
Unto the very ears of God:
'My brother was no keeper.'

It started then but did not stop,
And has not stopped by baths and drops,
To gush and froth a crimson blot,
On every family's crypt and plot.
The rancid pool flows deeper.

Not deep enough with guns and bombs,
Or filled up with a holocaust.
The blood that runs won't be enough,
Till to our wrath, we have succumbed.
All life becoming cheaper.

We're nothing in our neighbor's heart:
The hurting hurt for love that is naught,
All predators hunt till everyone's gone.
No soul is exempted of Satan or God,
From the hand of his fellow reaper.

But since the bloodshed had begun,
From the dawn of mankind's early sun,
God knew his own must one day run,
Through wounds in his afflicted son.
Of blood would come a redeemer.

From courts above to the cross of wood,
The God-man hung, redemption stood.
And dropped from him to all the world,
To every soul who has ever heard,
His blood cov'ring us forever!

BRING ON
THE DREAM

*"I will pour out my spirit upon all flesh; and **your sons
and your daughters shall prophesy, your old men shall
dream dreams, your young men shall see visions.**"*
– Joel 2:28

Bring on the dream, the beauty of me;
My purest potential that's yet to be seen.
A personal gift from God in me,
The best of my soul, bring on the dream!

Away with the reasons of why I'm afraid,
And all my excuses and former mistakes.
I'm deaf to the critics who always say nay,
Visiting all, but with me, they won't stay.

Bring on the dream! Why have it at all,
If not to respond and answer the call?
Not moving today is choosing to stall,
Choosing to quit, choosing to fall.

All that we really own in this life,
Are the dreams of our heart, the fires inside.
The choice that we have is to quench them or fight,
To dwell in our dark or live in the light.

AS SURE AS
YOU CAN

"...Ye have a watch: go your way,
*make it **as sure as you can**."*
Matthew 27:65

The tomb of Christ they sealed up fast;
But Pilate knew it wouldn't last.
Still, he let them work and plan:
Make it sure, as sure as you can.

So, they did with stones and guards,
And a tale to tell if things went wrong.
All to deny Christ's rise from the dead,
You have a watch, be as sure as you can.

The stone was rolled as a leaf in the wind;
The guards not impeding the Lord's ascent.
Their story's become a mockery since.
So much for the plans of men.

Today it's the same. We continue the game,
Denying his rise or ever he came.
Certain that we won't see him again,
And comfortable with this plan.

To the train of thought that God is naught,
Many have boarded. Many have bought,
The notion knowledge is really God,
And found inside each man.

But there is to each a time to die,
And a day when all, at last, shall find,
Despite the tries to hide his life,
The Lord rose, as he said.

For that day, are you prepared?
Better be sure, as sure as you can.

SET MY LIFE
TO MUSIC

"To the chief musician, a psalm of David."
Psalms 4-6,8,9,11-14,18-22,31,36,39,40,41,51-
62,64,65,68-70,109,139,140

David's testimony set to music as portrayed in the psalms.

Set my life to music; tell my story to the world.
Let the timing teach the crowds
of all I did and learned.
Make my life a passion of a song that can be felt,
A soul to be remembered, breathed
in by someone else.

Let the lyrics never lie of where I won and fell,
Rising to my triumphs and my failures quick to tell.
Harmonize the story with my
love, and love I spurned.
Set it all to music, see me shine, and see me burn.

Feel my pain and apathy, my virtue and my sin.
Move to the rhythm that is me, and
you'll know where I've been.
Hear my greatest heartaches, and my
greatest dreams come true.
Set my life to music, and you'll
learn I'm just like you.

NO, NOT WITH CHAINS

*". . . no man could bind him, **no, not with chains:**"*
- Mark 5:3

No, not with chains could the maniac crazed,
Be brought into sanity's 'sylum.
Nor tombs as his home and fetters for clothes,
Calm the fear of the villagers round him.

No, not with chains was the lunatic laid,
At the feet of the Savior writhing.
Nor by a tool in his hand did the Lord command,
The devils expelled in their crying.

No, not with chains was the maniac tamed,
And brought into soundness of mind.
But one catch of his eye beholding the Christ,
Infused a nature divine!

So is it today that peoples' mores,
Cannot be controlled by our means.
Shackle us fast in societal pacts,
And we all still do as we please.

No, not with chains can we put from our face
The evils of civilization.
The sins of the heart are not made to depart
By legal applications.

No, not with chains can we be remade
Nor cleansed from the sins of our race;
It is grace from the Lord, and the love that we show
That frees both man and state.

4.19

*"But my God shall supply **all your need** according to his riches in glory by Christ Jesus." – Philippians 4:19*

When pain becomes too much to
bear, and conflicts torture me,
Then is sent some arbiter to be my 4:19.
When that which satisfies men's
lives in my eyes can't be seen,
Some wondrous peace then fills
the void to be my 4:19.

When hope defers to a mind enflamed
with a sense of endless grief,
Then comes some friend, or news,
or 'luck' to be my 4:19.
Even in deep loneliness for a soul-mate out of reach,
The Lord becomes a comforter, Himself, my 4:19.
We never know from day to day
what will be our greatest need,
But we know when the needs do
come, God's prepared a 4:19.

BUT

"*But* ...."
– *I Kings 11:1*

Imagine every place you go that you already know,
Your mind was the best within it.
That was his mind, unequaled and bright,
But Solomon loved many women.

If seeing one day all the problems you faced,
Were resolved with your acumen,
Then you've sampled a tad of the wisdom he had.
But Solomon loved many women.

Think of what wealth could care for yourself,
And the families of thousands of men.
You'll then know the girth of his natural worth.
But Solomon loved many women.

When all over the world people follow your word,
And to you is the final say given,
Then wonder in awe at the leader he was!
But Solomon loved many women.

All that he made, everything he became,
For the profit of earth and heaven,
Now worthless and naught to this passionate heart,
Whose only love was to love many women.

HOME

"But now they desire a better country, that is, an heavenly:
wherefore God is not ashamed to be called their God:
for he hath prepared for them a city." – Heb. 11:16

When wondering, wandering back from war
And the battles of the day,
Let the pathway lead to a place of peace,
To thence from whence I came:
My Home.

Travelling far to accomplish some
Goal that I had set,
May the way be plain to return again
To where my heart has never left:
My Home.

When straying, straining my soiled soul
In the vices I pursued,
And once cast forth as dust to dirt,
I return to heal my wounds
At Home.

Begged, besot, beseeched by friends
To forsake my kind abode,
I see remained when they fall away
What I needed all along:
My Home.

A citizen sheer, though not of here
Nor of any land I've trod.
But past last breath, I'll know my rest
And see by the face of God,
I'm Home.

BE STILL

"Stand in awe, and sin not: commune with your
*own heart upon your bed, and **be still**. Selah"*
— Psalm 4:4

Be still my self-destructive soul, o why can't you be still?
There's no need to throw away the promise you've been given,
Or for you to burn away the bridges you have built.
Don't waste on earth that which you
know is to be stored in heaven,
Perceiving that the earthly things your heart will never fill.
Pursue them not lest you be from your best potential riven.

Be still my lonely soul; be thou very still.
In those who love you confide and share.
Go not to the error of drink and pills,
But of flesh and blood who care.
Beware the hurt and pain you feel,
When you think that no one's there.

Be still my raging soul, be still!
Hold sanity by a thread.
Don't let the fears and shrills,
Of warring voices in your head.
Strip you of your living will,
And bring you to the dead.

Still soul, be still.
We know in the end.
There's a God who will,
Make a joyful end.

Be still my soul.

COMING FOR
THY WORDS

*"Thy words were heard, and I am **come for thy words**."*
— *Daniel 10:12*

Overlapping conversations,
In a well-connected world,
All we want is one to care,
And listen to our words.

When in days of deep despair,
The greatest need is to be heard:
That one might hear and understand,
And be there for our words.

In the endless search for love,
For companionship we yearn.
To empathize, and feel, and share,
A kinship with our words.

When we go into our closets with
Bleeding hearts and shut the door,
Abiding there we find again,
Someone waiting for our words.

OF SERVANTS
AND SONS

"*And because ye are sons, God hath sent forth the Spirit of his Son into your hearts, crying, Abba, Father.* **Wherefore thou art no more a servant, but a son**; *and if a son, then an heir of God through Christ. Howbeit then, when ye knew not God, ye did service unto them which by nature are no gods. But now, after that ye have known God, or rather are known of God, how turn ye again to the weak and beggarly elements, whereunto ye desire again to be in bondage? Ye observe days, and months, and times, and years.* **I am afraid of you**, *lest I have bestowed upon you labour in vain.*"

– Galatians 4:6 – 11

How much the church has done,
Oiled well the business runs.
As each soul a stat's become,
So as CEOs we've won,
And staff--but not as sons.

What wealth of goods are sold:
The merch, the books, the songs!
So, from the flock procured,
Are funds for debts incurred.
We're merchants more than sons.

We keep a godly form,
In impressive speech and cloth;
Denying the power thereof,
While bidding masses, come,
Like sepulchers, not sons.

I fear the course we run:
Proving worth to God,
Working to be loved,
Defined by what we've done,
As servants, not as sons.

RESILIENCE

"For we can do nothing against the truth,
but for the truth." — II Cor. 13:8

Truth gives place, but stays the same; no
mind the games, no mind the fame.
Allows itself to be renamed, to be
defamed; revised again, again, again.
Youth train their brains to rewrite things;
renew things, explain mores in different
ways. No mind the games, no mind the fame.
Truth remains the same, unchanged.

One day, they say, will be made plain the
truth we've let lay waste today and paid no
mind in mindless haste to find a fate for
which we say is better cause to live today.
But there's no way to overstate what truth will try to
say, exclaim! Though trace on deafened ears it may.
What we say can't be rephrased, yesterday
can't be remade. The way it staged and how
it played will always stay, no mind games, no
mind the day. Truth is truth and will remain.

SAFE AND SOUND

"Thy brother is come; and thy father hath killed the fatted
*calf, because he hath received him **safe and sound**."*
- Luke 15:27

A son and glad inheritor of his
father's hard-earned gains,
Journeyed, not with purpose, but
intemperance in his veins.
Far his destination, not a place but out from power,
Weakened, as he wandered, as
a dis-engrafted flower.

Dissipative was his substance,
Dissipative was his spending.
Dissipative was his life, as all licentious living--
Ascended, eviscerated, as an incense to the sky.
His wealth went to the ether, his soul not far behind.

Famine came (it always comes) as fire in a forge,
To purge the land of plenty and of
men their feigned cohorts.
When thus the son was wanton, he
took work against his soul,
And toiled as a bondman, and as a son no more.

Depraved, alone, and desperate he
communed with one he could,
Wiping the refuse from his face,
before himself, he stood.
And recalled that in another land,
at another time gone by,
Whatever discontent he had; he
at least had had—a life.

Though both time and substance
were now forever sifted,
Still, his life was in him. Still, a
chance he had been gifted.
To come back home—where he was
loved—his error to expound,
And be welcomed back again, a
son, now safe and sound.

A son I am, we are, have been, who
have from our perches fluttered,
Fell at last in our journeys forth
to be set free of others.
Let us convene with the one soul left,
ourselves, to come around,
And remember those who'll love us
and embrace us, safe and sound.

ARE WE NOT ALL SIN?

"For there is none righteous, no not one." – Romans 3:10
"For all have sinned, and come short of
the glory of God." – Romans 3:23

Are we not all vanity, are we not all sin?
Even the very best of men show oft their frailty,
Not just by course but daily! Are we not all sin?

Who is to be trusted? What can we believe?
All are given to deceit, seeking what we've lusted.
Each by idols left disgusted. All hollow—so are we.

Exists there any character to do right in the dark,
Or are we all just marked, by vices and past err?
All have bitten on those lures,
ensnaring our own hearts.

There are no more heroes, perhaps have never been.
Each one has failed or fallen, so
the human story goes.
Never virtue have we known. Are we not all sin?

Best it is to tread this sod in a
state of grace and humbly.
Best to go on slowly lest we stumble as we trod.
Best to heed the words of God who
gives grace unto the lowly.

DEPTHS OF GRACE

"But Noah found grace in the eyes
of the Lord." – Genesis 6:8

All forthwith to be destroyed,
one man found a gift:
The first of its kind to spare his
life and of his closest kin.
Blessed to weather the wrath to come
that doomed his fellow man,
Presumed to be a lucky one,
availed in grace's plan:

Grace to know a hundred years the
world would be undone,
Ample time to see the doom
of everyone he loved.
Sufficient were those days to
warn; deficient for reform,
Compounding grief in Noah's heart
each day he was ignored.

Grace that set him laboring hard
for ternion generations,
Splintered, bloodied, sore, and worn
for a vessel's fabrication.
Carpentry to build the ark, husbandry to conserve.
Biology for what the Lord had sent him to preserve.
Philanthropist to do the task,
psychologist for his kin,
Onerous weights for ten to bear
were placed upon one man.

Grace that threw him forty days on
the sea of eternity's storm,
Bade him house a thousand beasts for
a hundred and twenty more.
Haunted by the claws and shrills of
fading souls beneath the surf,
Amplified and echoed in each
wave that struck the door.
His ancient bones preserved to bear
the pangs of building earth,
Succumbed at last to misery, he
fled to wine and mirth.
When he disembarked he found
naught but swampy ground.
"Perhaps, methinks," in a lapse of faith,
"Grace what let them drown."

This we find the first-time grace
is etched in sacred script;
Simply giving man a chance to labor, love, and live.
Requited with the smile of God
when he took the gift and did.
Grace that gives us hope and
space to fully live today,
And not devoid of hardships as
would TV preachers say.
Learn it well from Noah's life
the nature of this grace,
Life is hard but rewarding still, as
God grants time and place.

HAVE WE
NO KING?

*"In those days there was **no king** in Israel: every man did*
that which was right in his own eyes" – Judges 21:25

A wayward maid for a price she named,
Sold herself for naught;
Some willing men with lustful hands,
Acquired what shouldn't be bought,
We pay for abhorrent flings.

The adulterous wife had sold her life,
Back to her old profession.
Her selfish dad, glad her he had,
Minded not the marriage concession.
As long as it's good for me.

A drunken pair, their revelries shared,
For the greater part of a week.
Till the hasty man with a foolish plan,
Led his wife to jeopardy,
The moment is all we see.

Their wrong decision this city to visit,
Was wicked in all the worst ways.
Lecherous men in carnal sin,
Demanded the man to rape!
Against lust there is no creed.

The conniving men with selfish intent,
Devised a cowardly plot:
Send the maids for abuse and rape,
And see if they live or not.
Whose was the greater greed?

A widower's pain o'er hurt and sin,
Cut her dead body apart,
To denounce and cry to every tribe,
"You've no ruler in your hearts!"
No one had a king.

There was no king a peace to bring,
Or direct the nation's mores.
No guiding hand to stay the land,
From utter moral decay.
Was it true there was no king?

Or is it that the grief that passed
Lay not in regal want.
But was due to a King they knew,
But one whom they forgot?

Perhaps our woes, like those ago,
That stay with us even yet.
Are not due to a King not come,
But to one we do reject.
Do we have no King?

ANOTHER LAW

Paul confronts his own humanity.

*"For I delight in the law of God after the inward man: But I see **another law** in my members, warring against the law of my mind, and bringing me into captivity to the law of sin which is in my members."*
– Romans 7:22, 23

My brother, I would help thee and
succor thee in life's way,
To reach your full potential and have victory today.
But another law I see: the one of my own envy.
Fearing your success, cheering your duress,
My helping hand is stayed, another
law I have obeyed.

My sister, I should uphold you in the holiest esteem,
To regard you in great honor and provide security.
But another law is found: intemperance abounds.
Sanctity I've shunned; a predator I've become.
Honor now displaced, another law I have obeyed.

My family, I should guide you
to the favor of the Lord,
To partake of all the goodness that
he promised in his Word.
But another law's put forth: to
love the present world.
Having what I must, and delivered to my lust,
I have guided you astray; another
law I have obeyed.

My Savior, I could love thee-- be a living sacrifice,
Putting no one else above thee,
counting you the highest prize.
But another I esteem: the law of loving me.
Regarding no one but myself,
there's no room for any else.
My God I have replaced. Another law I have obeyed.

Another law I have obeyed, if not the law of God,
Other judgments I have made that
I should not make at all.
God's will he hath decreed; his tenets will I heed?
Forsaking mine own heart, His
commandments to impart,
Lest I be a castaway, the law of God I must obey!

LIVING TODAY

"Redeeming the time, because the days
are evil." - Ephesians 5:16

Although I may not die today,
The day will die to me.
And with it goes my surest chance,
To sway eternity.

Today has come without regard–
In utter apathy,
And cares not how I cross its path,
To fail or to succeed.

It marches to its resting place,
No matter how I've lived.
It bids adieu forever more,
With no more grace to give.

If I'm to make a difference then,
I better do it now,
Not waiting for another day,
That may not come around.

Although I may not die today,
So too I may not live.
For life is not just having life,
But living life to give.

FROM HIMSELF

". . . A good man shall be satisfied from
himself." - Proverbs 14:14

The labors done; the glory won,
From the contests of the day.
But fades too fast with the moment past,
And bothers not to stay.
Was the passion worth it, the toil and the zeal,
To elicit man's profession of my
praise from 'neath my heel?
The praise goes with their breath, gone before it left.
I worked so hard for this. Is it the reason that I live?

The friends gone home;
my highs made low,
Since the revelry dispensed.
We had a blast--loud, now past.
My conscience alone remains.
Did the friends stay longer when
I lost myself with them?
Did they rather not pass faster when
I'd nothing left to give?
Their closeness never came,
approached then fled away.
Shallow favor was my wish. And
I live my life for this?

My goals achieved, all that I dreamed!
But now leanness in my soul?
I had my thrill but am not fulfilled,
No remedy to be whole.
Was the lust so lovely as to chase away remorse?
Could I not foresee that in the
end, I would be worse?
Satisfaction is the wind-- felt but not retained.
Chasing passing bliss, is this the reason that I live?

May this thought avail a better version of myself:
That a life lived to the fullest must
be lived for someone else.

ALL OF MY CARE

"Casting all your upon him; for he careth for you"
- I Peter 5:7

All of my care did he say?
As though it was but a light thing.
The sum of one's fears to lay,
At the feet of a caring King.

All of **my** care did he mean?
Proprietary fears of mine,
That worry no one but me,
Are worthy of his time?

All of my **care** heaved forth,
The grievous, and silly, and just.
Somehow to him, they are worth,
His hearing when spew them I must.

Yes, all of my care did he say!
To share in their load he intends,
And further to take them away,
When I call on my faithful Friend.

All of my cares can be gone,
With peace coming into their place.
Given by a gracious God,
When for my cares, I care to pray.

LOVE IS STRONG AS DEATH

"For love is strong as death...." – Song of Songs 8:6
A Shakespearean Sonnet

O set me as a seal upon thine heart.
Which never could a force of earth unset,
An everlasting token that thou art
The object of my love—as strong as death.
Alas I have from you been far removed.
Upon our days as one the sun has set.
Yet still reverberates a love that moves,
To you across the span—as strong as death.
Caressing and reminding you of truth:
My love is not so fragile to be stilled,
Nor frail that ought can have it be removed.
In parting, love exerts a stronger will!

The echoes of my life to you are sent,
Remember me, my love, as strong as death.

THE COLOR
OF LIMA

*"And when he was come near, he beheld the
city, and wept over it." - Luke 19:41*

Written on the Pacific Ocean during a mission trip to Lima

What is your color Lima Perú,
And what will you be in posterity's view?
A city contrived in contrasting hues.
What is that color, O Lima Perú?

In the prism of progress, you're both first and third:
A commerce that's growing but masses who hurt.
Free trade or oppression, which will you choose?
On economy's pallet, what is your hue?

In society's spectrum, your span's a great length—
Imported influence and cultural strength.
Unchanged or unhindered, tradition or new,
What color of culture, O Lima Peru?

The dichotomy's strong in eternity's view:
A knowledge of God, but has he knowledge of you?
When the Word of God grows here in Lima Perú,
And your hearts are exposed to its life-giving hue,
In that moment of time your true colors we'll view,
When with the gospel of Christ,
you decide what to do.
Is it a shade of repentance, O Lima Perú?

The Coast of Lima, Peru

INJUSTICE

"Doth God pervert judgment? Or doth the
Almighty pervert justice?" – Job 8:3

When God perverts his justice,
what are people left to do?
Not perverse as though he sins. But
in the sense that justice skews
With views that seems to make no
sense and are logically inverted,
How can we believe a truth
perceived to be subverted?

It's not right that millions die when leaders disagree,
And brothers suffer martyrs' plights
while we live peacefully.
Why do the wicked rise to rule
the lands of people good,
And hateful peoples raise their fists
against their brotherhood?

I cannot grasp the apathy over evils we engender,
Nor can I see that for the weak,
there be any just defender.
I can find no pattern to the victims cancer takes,
Or reasons that diseases often
hurt the sweetest saints.

Sometimes, I've learned, you can't
discern Satan's work from God's,
Or in the moment from which
one the fiery trials come.
But going on I turn to see that in the path behind,
Whatever imps' or man's intent,
God's been faithful in my life.

The ills of life confound me as
they do my fellow men.
Yet when God perverts his justice,
it is not for truth to bend.
But rather for my pride to break
and to his ways repent,
So that when I do not understand,
I go on trusting him.

FIRST ALTAR

"And Saul built an altar unto the Lord: the same
was the first altar that he built unto the Lord."
- I Samuel 14:35

After all my heroes fall, and true love goes away,
Or after all my health is gone when
the strength of youth decays;
Maybe when regrets surpass the
good I've done in life,
Or once I've lost my family to
abuse, or vice, or strife;
Maybe when my children grow and
make my same mistakes,
Or when my money and my time
I've squandered all away;
When all my life is finally done,
and I realize it's too late,
Maybe then I'll think, repent, and
an altar to God I'll make.

PERSUADED

*"Then Agrippa said unto Paul, Almost thou
persuadest me to be a Christian. And Paul said,
I would to God, that not only thou, but also all
that hear men this day, were both **almost, and
altogether** such as I am, except these bonds."*
— Acts 26:28, 29

There's more to me than mistake and disgrace;
There's potential for the image of God in my face.
Right and the wrong in my mind plead their case.
Almost but not altogether.

I run for God, but it's uphill track,
A parachute of sin and wind on my back.
I want to let loose, but I still hold back.
Almost but not altogether.

I want to give it all, but I don't want to drain.
I want to win the race, but I don't want to train.
I want to be better while staying the same.
Almost but not altogether.

Search me O God and know my heart.
Make every wicked, evil way to depart.
My life's in your hands, tell me where do I start?
Almost and Altogether.

ALLUREMENT

"Love not the world, neither the things that are in the world. If any man love the world, the love of the Father is not in him..." – I John 2:15

The world's ahead outrunning us, outgaining us,
And calling back it speaks to us:
"Catch up to us and be with us,
Enjoying all there is to life on earth."

Arrogantly, because we lust,
Think we are eternity's cusp.
Believe that all the world is thus,
Spinning to give us mirth.

That somehow all that's shown to us,
And promised us can once be ours.
And once it is twill be enough,
To fill our sense of worth.

But pursuing lust it dawns on us,
To some of us when life is dusk.
The world's a ruse, it's not enough.
Our void's a spiritual dearth.

LIMITS OF GOD

*"**Wait** on the Lord: be of good courage, and he shall strengthen thine heart: **wait, I say**, on the Lord."*
– Psalm 27:14

To the mountains, stay;
To wild wolves, bay;
To ocean tides, sway;
To the seed, decay;
To light, form a ray;
To grass, grow in blades;
To the wind, give way.

To God all obey,
Except when he'll say,
To his own children, wait.

BAWLING SAUL
*"And Saul eyed David from that day
and forward." – I Samuel 18:9*

Might and a name I was cravin',
But now I seek a lost haven.
Was the king of war,
But alas, no more.
How I loathe the man they call David!

TESTIMONY
*"The woman then left her waterpot, and went her way
into the city, and saith to the men, Come, see a man,
which told me all things that ever I did: is not this
the Christ?"– John 4:28-29*

She went to draw from the well,
And met with the Lord for a spell.
She then went away,
A different way than she came,
The miracles of God to tell!

SIMPLE CONVERSION
*"Except ye be converted, and become as little
children, ye shall not enter into the kingdom
of heaven." - Matthew 18:3*

He said to a child, just come!
When up to his lap he had sprung,
He told all around,
That heaven is found,
By doing what this boy has done!

THE KINGDOM
OF MEN

"This matter is by the decree of the watchers, and the
demand by the word of the holy ones: to the intent
that the living may know that the most High ruleth
*in the **kingdom of men**, and giveth it to whomsoever*
he will, and setteth up over it the basest of men."
- Daniel 4:17

He was august in the realm of men;
powerful, evil, fearful king.
Molding a likeness wrought in gold
where people would bow and sing.
The armies of the crescent, his; its
caches of wealth and food.
Even Daniel, inspired of God,
ascribed it an age of gold.

But in the height of hubris came
the humbler for his heart,
The morrow's golden rays to make
the golden king corrupt.
He spurned the seer, and prophecy sneered.
But in what are named his silent years,
Nebuchadnezzar's psyche morphed,
His palace now a sanatorium.

The might of his sword brought to scratch;
his commands reduced to drivel,
As regal as his gauntly robe stained
of dung and spittle.
For seven years, insanity's slave, and
emerging from the cloud,
Acknowledged God for all he'd done.
The king, at last, had bowed.
God called the man his servant,
accomplishing all his will,
Far removed from former wants of
choosing to rape and kill.

Today we lament over whom we elect.
We preach and debate, their power resent.
Nebuchadnezzar, we're quick to forget.
The Most High still rules in the kingdom of men.

"SORRY IS NOTHING"

"For he found no place of repentance, though he sought it carefully with tears." – Hebrews 12:17

There's nothing to write and nothing to say,
No retraction for some ways we behave.
There's not a rewind, delete, or undo.
In life, there's just play and stop
when you're through.
Young soul, beware of some risks you may take,
When there's nothing to write,
and nothing to say.

WHAT IS TRUTH?

"…To this end was I born, and for this cause came
I into the world, that I should bear witness unto
the truth. Every one that is of the truth heareth
my voice. Pilate saith unto him, **what is truth?"**
— *John 18:37, 38*

His time to die now drawing nigh,
the Lord decided to impart
Into the ruler's hardened heart,
the notion there is truth.
Not could be, or shades of gray or
maybe if you think that way,
But verily there is a way to know that there is truth.

The words alit upon his ears as
he bristled, and he jeered,
Caring not to know or hear of existential truth.
Pilate sealed his fate that day and could
not to this thought be swayed.
Rather repent, he chose debate and
proffered 'What is truth?'

I accept in life all that I feel and expect
my mind to make it real;
Only to my heart I kneel, and tell myself that's truth.
Pilate, in myself I find. I fight
his battles in my mind,
And try to tell myself I'm right. But
we both know there is truth.

THIS MAN

"Then came the officers to the chief priests and Pharisees;
and they said unto them, Why have ye not brought him?
*The officers answered, Never man spake like **this man**."*
- John 7:45, 46

Never man spake like this man,
never a statesman as just.
Never a truth so honest or needed nearly as much.
Never a passion so piercing, or
compassion so understood.
Never man spake like this man,
never a man so good.
Never man spake like this man,
never a boldness as strong,
Never a great one so humble,
never a brief life so long.

Never so silent one's critics or
confounded his haters could be.
Never so blameless a virtue that
would validate one's speech.
Never man spake like this man, who
by all of creation, is served.
Never one to come again with
expressions to change the world.
Never man spake like this man.
There is no one like the Lord!

REDEMPTION

"Howbeit the hairs of his head began to grow again…."
— Judges 16:22

A life of strength, stronger in death,
That conquered though conquered by sin.
Regrets he had and errors, yet,
His hair did grow again.

Enormous potential power,
'Til human nature intervened.
And shaved the promise from his head,
And with it all his dreams.

Your destiny changed; life rearranged.
A different course you had to chart.
But stand up strong and face head-on,
The new future that you start.

Live not in past failures,
But in hope of redemption's plan:
You're forgiven and given grace.
These hairs will grow again.

MY TARRIED CLOUD

*"And when the **cloud tarried** long upon the tabernacle
many days, then the children of Israel kept the charge
of the Lord, and journeyed not." – Numbers 9:19*

"It should happen any minute now,
That God will lift this tarried cloud,
And carry us to Canaan very soon."
But days all passed till months were found,
Without any movement of the cloud.
And the camp all thought, "the
Lord, he must not love you."

Never moving, hope was losing,
Never seeing, not believing.

Then in a timing all his own,
The still, small voice from before the throne
Descended and the cloud, it started movin.
The race, it wasn't theirs to run,
No, the pace was His who had begun
The wondrous notion, there's a God who loves you.

Never moving, hope was losing,
Never seeing, not believing.

And so, their trials and time God set,
As He does today, but we still forget
The movements of the Lord are at His cue.
The tarried clouds of doubt I face,
Tire my soul like the Hebrew race.
But I'll learn at last to trust the
words 'God loves you!'

Ever-growing, hope is gleaming!
Not yet seeing but believing!

CANDLE LIGHT

"Thou wilt light my candle...." – *Psalm 18:28*

Light a candle God, an inspiration in my life;
Any movement, anything, so I'll believe in light.
Light a candle God, if only a spark of faith;
Just a stirring of my soul. Your existence, validate!

Light the candle God for the next steps of my life.
Let me see enough to hope,
enough to do what's right.
A lamplight for my wandering steps
to keep me in thy beam,
Light my candle, God, that I fulfill your will, me.

Light the candle God, of your
Word within my heart,
Let it flicker, fan, and flame.
Finish in me what you start!
Guide me to my resting place
one day beside my sword,
Living to my fullest in the glory of thy Word.

THE SPEED
OF LIFE

"And Jacob served seven years for Rachel; and
they seemed unto him but a few days, for the
love he had to her." – Genesis 29:20

On a ride of light, my life must be,
Destined to pass before it's seen,
Gone ere my lips could say I breathed,
For the love I have for thee.

My days pass as the morning dew,
As water through a stream.
And accelerate each day with you,
For the love I have for thee.

Life goes slow when you're alone;
Love's what brings the speed!
Guess I'll be gone before you know,
All the love I have for thee.

THY GENTLENESS

"Thy gentleness hath made me great." Psalm 18:35

Your example is a beacon of how life is to be lived,
But future me can't fit into the model that you give.
I'll stumble in depression or excel you in my pride.
A pattern then is not enough to
bring greatness to a life.

Being tutored by your lessons
was a master education,
Doing wonders for my acumen—
but not in application.
Instruct me in your wisdom, but
I may not use it right.
Education then is not the key to greatness in a life.

Your wise reproofs are needed more
than I would dare admit.
But ease your hand, I'll fail you;
be too hard, I'll quit.
Corrections only last as long as I let them have a say,
Proving with rejection rules alone
can't make me great.

But looking back I recollect the
best of qualities in you:
Patient understanding, a compassionate world view.
Forgiving and forgetting faults,
restoring me in grace.
In the end, it was your gentleness
that propelled me to be great.

FEAR NO EVIL

*"I will **fear no evil**, for **thou art with me**."*
Psalm 23:4

"I 'm fearful Lord," I said to God,
"I'll always be alone."
He answered back, "You've never
been. Fear not and go on."
I said, "life's overwhelming me.
I'm breaking for the stress."
"Care only for your load today
and trust me for the rest."
"What about my frailties God? Of
my weakness I'm afraid.

That my sin will one day overcome

and make me disobey."

For this, his words were subtle, as

his Spirit spoke instead,

That it was He, who helps me fight

the battles in my head.

I spoke of family, friends, and jobs,

of troubles that befall.

For each of these, he said to me,

"You've naught to fear at all."

It seems when life is at its worst, and

my soul has come undone,

I remember all I truly need: Thou

art with me is enough.

INDEX OF INSIGHTS

Here you will find the literary devices and tools used to create some of the poems in this book.

ALLUREMENT

This poem is intentionally euphonic, carrying the S and U sounds throughout, as an alluring chant or spell. Such is the constant pull of the world's temptations on each of our hearts. The premise is carried further by the serpentine layout of the poem, to depict a serpent's sliver.

ARE WE NOT ALL SIN?

The internal and end rhyme scheme is intentionally transposed in each line to convey shortcomings and flaws, which is the theme of the poem. So instead of the middle and end of a line rhyming with the middle and end of the next line, the middle of the first line rhymes with the end of the second line, while the end of the first line rhymes with the middle of the second line. This perhaps makes the poem confusing, complicated, and inefficient. Such is the effect of sin on our lives.

BAWLING SAUL, TESTIMONY, SIMPLE CONVERSION

These poems are limericks, short poems with a defined meter and rhyme structure. Bawling Saul was the first scripture poem I ever wrote, at the age of twelve.

BE STILL

Written in a diminishing syllabic format to portray the speaker calming down as the poem goes on, or learning to be still if you will, until at the end there is very little left to say. It symbolizes our own lives and emotions. When troubles arise, we first tend to be vehement and raw in our emoting, but with time and grace, we learn not to overreact and to trust God to bring us through the trial on his terms, and in his way.

BLOOD TOUCHETH BLOOD

You will find this poem flowing with a constant use of the 'uh' and 'oh' sounds, as in the word blood, to audibly portray the title and subject of the poem, that of blood flow, both human and divine. It was also written in a darker tone to denote the distinct contrast between humanity's failures and God's grace to overcome those failures.

THE COLOR OF LIMA

This poem was drafted while I was on a visit to Lima Peru, as I sat along its Pacific Ocean coast. The picture was taken on the coast overlooking the Pacific Ocean and Lima's famous Lighted Cross.

FROM HIMSELF

This poem, among others, uses parallelism to emphasize key points within the poem. Parallelism is using different words in similar structure or meter to echo the same concept.

The Bible itself uses parallelism abundantly. (Psalm 19, verses 7 – 9 are a classic example of parallelism.)

In fact, when portions of the Bible are referred to as poetry it is because those passages utilize this literary device that can survive translation between languages. Whereas other poetic tools that were used to write portions of the Bible, such as rhyme and acrostics, are not apparent in English translations. But thankfully, we can still observe and enjoy the artistry of written scripture in our own language because of the use and preservation of parallelism in those scriptures.

INJUSTICE

This poem seeks to incorporate the themes of the book of Job itself: despair, doubt, questioning, and ultimately, trusting God even when the answers to life's problems are not clear.

LIMITS OF GOD

Written with as few words as possible to mirror the substance of God's words at creation, where the great power of his words were in full display. He not only said very little to create the universe (let there be), but he also speaks very succinctly and directly when telling us about it in the Genesis account of creation.

Another uniqueness of this poem is that, while its structure imitates God's powerful words, its content points out how sadly dismissive we as people can be of those words while the rest of his creation obeys. This is why all lines of the poem are five syllables, representing the first five days of creation, while the last line dealing with mankind is six syllables, representing the sixth day of creation when God made us.

LOVE IS STRONG AS DEATH

The Song of Songs (Solomon) is the love letter book of the Bible, depicting the romance shared between a bride and her groom. And while the theme is allegorical of the love between Christ and his church, the story as is should not be overlooked for its mastery of capturing the raw emotions felt between two lovers. As such, this poem was written in the format of a Shakespearean sonnet, said to be the most romantic of all poetic styles.

MY TARRIED CLOUD
This poem is written to be read at a slow place, related to the themes of the poem itself of longing and waiting.

PERSUADED
This poem was written to be read in a faster pace, perhaps at rap song speed, to symbolize the struggle to decide one's commitment level to Christ, which is most common and most ardent while we're young.

REDEMPTION
Sampson's name was intentionally omitted from this poem because the theme of his life transcends his life. Failure, suffering, regrets, overcoming, etc. These are qualities found in each of our lives and should not be conceptually ascribed to a select few. The story of Samson is not given to us for entertainment, though it

certainly is that, but as Paul said, such stories are given to us for our admonishment, on whom the ends of the world are come. We are all Sampson at times to some degree or another.

SET MY LIFE TO MUSIC

Each psalm has some amount of introductory information accompanying it before the psalm begins. Almost like a user's guide, this information provides insight into the nature or context of that particular psalm. Once such introductory statement found before many of David's psalms is the phrase, 'to the chief musician'. This phrase implies that whatever was about to be written was to be put to music by the temple's musicians and taught to the people as a song so they would remember what was written. In other words, these are psalms that were intentionally made public and emphasized to the masses. And deemed important enough to be remembered, were set to music for that purpose.

The fascinating thing about this is the fact that many of the psalms that David instructed to be made public were intensely personal in nature, revealing many weaknesses of his own soul, such as doubt, fear, and bitterness. Some even depicted embarrassing and hurtful personal failures, such as his adultery with Bathsheba. David's humility and devotion to God allowed him to use his own life story, the good and the bad, as a tool to encourage and educate those around him. He taught his testimony to others that they may learn valuable life lessons. It is that truth that inspired this poem. May we all be reminded by the life of David just how powerful our personal testimonies can be.

SORRY IS NOTHING

The title of this poem is derived from a life experience of my youth. A personal failure hurt some people close to me. As I tried apologizing to one of them who was particularly hurt, the direct quote I received from them is the title of this poem. And they were right. I immediately thought about the scripture passage coinciding with this poem, and later drafted the poem based on that passage and that experience.

SELECT QUOTES

Many poetry lovers, myself included, often enjoy select quotes or statements in a poem just as much, if not more than, the entire poem itself. For one, extracting a relatable truth from a piece of literature can be fulfilling, and two, memorizing a good line is so much easier than memorizing an entire poem! What's more, it is common for writers to create poems starting with just one line or one main thought, well before any structure or context is added, and then build the poem around that initial thought. Listed here are some aphoristic quotes from this volume:

Satisfaction is the wind, felt but not retained.
\- From Himself

Life goes slow when you're alone,
love's what brings the speed!
\- The Speed of Life

It seems when life is at its worst and
my soul has come undone,
God tells me all I truly need, 'thou art with me' is enough.
‒ Fear No Evil

Although I may not die today, so too I may not live.
For life is not just having life but living life to give.
‒ Living Today

My love is not so fragile to be stilled,
Nor frail that ought can have it be removed
In parting love exerts a stronger will!
‒ Love is Strong as Death

All that we really own in this life
Are the dreams of our heart, the fires inside.
The choice that we have is to quench them or fight,
To dwell in our dark, or live in the light.
‒ Bring on the Dream

Pilate in myself I find, I fight his battles
In my mind and try to tell myself I'm right.
But we both know there is truth.
– What is Truth

Going on I turn to see that in the path behind,
Whatever imps' or man's intent,
God's been faithful in my life.
– Injustice

ABOUT THE AUTHOR

Raised in West Virginia, William became a believer at the age of 10 through the ministry of Landmark Baptist Church. His faith journey continued from there to Chicagoland where he earned two theology degrees and worked in full-time ministry for over a decade. He wrote his first scripture poem at the age of 12 and continues that meditative practice to this day.

CPSIA information can be obtained
at www.ICGtesting.com
Printed in the USA
BVHW030906310720
585138BV00002B/4/J